Adventurous Spirit

A Story about Ellen Swallow Richards

by Ethlie Ann Vare

illustrations by Jennifer Hagerman

A Carolrhoda Creative Minds Book

Carolrhoda Books, Inc./Minneapolis

Most of the illustrations in this book are adapted from photographs taken of Ellen Richards throughout her lifetime. For the use of the original photographs which inspired Jennifer Hagerman's drawings, we would like to thank the MIT Museum and the Vassar College Library.

Text copyright © 1992 by Ethlie Ann Vare
Illustrations copyright © 1992 by Carolrhoda Books, Inc.

LIBRARY OF CONGRESS CATALOGING-IN-PUBLICATION DATA

Vare, Ethlie Ann.
    Adventurous spirit : a story about Ellen Swallow Richards / by
Ethlie Ann Vare ; illustrations by Jennifer Hagerman.
        p.   cm. — (A Carolrhoda creative minds book)
    Includes bibliographical references.
    Summary: A biography of Ellen Swallow Richards, the first woman
to study at the Massachusetts Institute of Technology, founder of the
American home economics movement, and first professional woman
chemist.
    ISBN 0-87614-733-3 (lib. bdg.)
    1. Richards, Ellen H. (Ellen Henrietta), 1842-1911—Juvenile literature.
2. Chemists—United States—Biography—Juvenile literature. 3. Women
chemists—United States—Biography—Juvenile literature. [1. Richards,
Ellen H. (Ellen Henrietta), 1842-1911. 2. Chemists. 3. Home economists.]
I. Hagerman, Jennifer, ill. II. Title. III. Series.
QD22.R48V37   1992
540'.92—dc20
[B]   91-39714
                                                                  CIP
                                                                   AC

Manufactured in the United States of America

1   2   3   4   5   6   97   96   95   94   93   92

Table of Contents

Author's Note

Peter Swallow was a courageous man.
"Where anyone else has been, there I can go,"
he used to say.
"This is not a bad working motto,"
answered his daughter, Ellen, many years later.
"But adventurous spirits go beyond this,
and do what has never been done before."

Ellen Henrietta Swallow Richards was an adventurous spirit who went where no one had gone before. She broke new ground and did things that no woman had ever done.

In the 1860s, at a time when few women went to high school, Ellen went to college. Despite many obstacles, she became the first woman to study at the Massachusetts Institute of Technology. Ellen Richards was the first professional woman chemist in the United States.

Not only did Ellen lead the way in the fields of water pollution and nutrition, but she also opened doors for other women. When she earned an advanced degree in chemistry, she showed that women were not too silly to learn science. When she worked while married, wore comfortable clothes, and ate simple and healthy foods, Ellen set an example for other women to follow. And follow they did.

History best remembers Ellen Richards as the founder of the American home economics movement. Today, "home economics" is considered an old-fashioned idea. But in Ellen's day, the idea of bringing science into the home was shocking. Women were not supposed to be smart enough to understand such things. Ellen's definition of home economics was that for a healthy, happy life, everyone should have fresh air, clean water, and pure food. She thought it was the job of scientists to bring these things to people.

If Ellen Richards were living now, we would call her a "consumer advocate" and an "environmentalist." There is nothing old-fashioned about her ideas at all. In her quiet, friendly way, Ellen was a revolutionary.

① A Great Deal of Work to Do

Fanny Swallow leaned out the kitchen door of the Massachusetts farmhouse and called her daughter's name one more time. Nellie? Nellie! Where could that girl be?

Ellen Henrietta Swallow—or Nellie, as everyone called her—was in her garden. She was straightening the rock border she had built for her plants. If her mother found out she had been lifting rocks...! That just wasn't fitting for a girl. Girls were supposed to stay indoors, helping their mothers cook and sew. If a doctor hadn't ordered Nellie to get lots of fresh air for her fragile health, she wouldn't be outside even now.

Nellie heard her mother call, but she took her time going back to the big, stuffy house. What was she going to have to do today? Scrub the kitchen table with sand until the wood was shiny as marble? Make tiny little stitches in a silly lace doily that would only catch dust on a corner table? Nellie could do "woman's work" as well as anyone, but it wasn't much fun.

Nellie Swallow would rather help her father drive the wagon. She could ride a horse and drive the cows into the barn as well as any boy she knew. She even liked pitching hay and cleaning the stables.

She would have loved to milk the cows, but her mother would never hear of that. It would ruin her ladylike hands, said Fanny.

Fanny called her daughter again. Time for lessons!

Lessons? Nellie stopped her dawdling and ran to the kitchen. Her mind raced at the thought of learning something new. What would it be today? Reading? Arithmetic? Latin? Fanny laughed as Nellie, her gray eyes wide with excitement, whirled into the room.

Fanny, a former schoolteacher, thought it was wonderful that Nellie was so quick, so curious.

With her husband, Peter, who divided his time between farming and teaching, Fanny gave their only child lessons at home.

Fanny was glad to have such an eager pupil. But sometimes she worried about Nellie. Most people in the middle 1800s didn't know what to make of a girl as clever as Nellie Swallow. Most people believed then that girls had smaller brains than boys and weren't capable of learning difficult things. A girl could never really understand logic or mathematics or science, they said.

Fanny and Peter Swallow knew better. Whenever Fanny—whose health was uncertain—felt up to it, she and Nellie would sit down to lessons in the kitchen after breakfast. It was Nellie's favorite time of the day.

As much as she enjoyed her garden (her botany lesson) and collecting the eggs in the henhouse (that was her biology), she always thought there was something special about seeing facts printed in a book. To Nellie, books were magic.

When Nellie was sixteen, her father decided to quit farming and open a general store. He moved the family to a larger town—Westford, Massachusetts—and set up shop. Nellie, so good with numbers, became his assistant.

If there were no customers to wait on, Nellie could always be found perched on a footstool near the potbellied stove, reading. If she took the horse-drawn streetcar to visit friends, she passed the time reading a book. Even if she was walking across the flower-lined town square, she had her nose buried in a book.

"You had better stop reading so much!" her uncle George would say. Uncle George liked it better when Nellie brought home ribbons from the county fair for her embroidery and her breadbaking. These were much more important skills for a girl, he thought. Like most men—and even women—of his day, Uncle George felt that education for women was a bad idea.

"What good does higher education do a woman?" asked the politicians. "Can she make a better pudding for it?" After all, most women in the 1860s married, had a family, and contented themselves cooking and cleaning for that family. If a woman wanted to have a profession, only a few jobs—in teaching, nursing, and a handful of other areas—were available.

If a bright girl like Nellie were lucky enough to earn money, then it legally belonged to her father or her husband or her older brother. By law, a woman didn't own the clothes on her back. And women couldn't elect new politicians to change these laws either, because women weren't allowed to vote.

Most people, Uncle George included, didn't understand Nellie's hunger for learning. But her parents did. They encouraged her to go to Westford Academy, a high school that accepted girls. (Many did not.) Nellie studied math, writing, French, and Latin.

In 1862, twenty-year-old Nellie Swallow graduated from Westford Academy. At that time in the United States, the Civil War was raging. Young men in Westford and other Northern towns joined the Union Army and headed South to bloody battles. Back in Massachusetts, their jobs were vacant. Nellie was offered a position as a schoolteacher and she accepted instantly.

She dreamed of doing more in this world than baking a better pudding. Being a schoolteacher was one way to follow her dreams. Unlike most girls of twenty, Nellie was in no hurry to marry. "The young or old gentleman has not yet made his appearance who can entice me away from my free and independent life," she confided to her favorite cousin, Annie.

As excited as Nellie was to take her new job, her body was too weak. She suffered one bout of measles, then another. "It was a severe disappointment," Nellie told Annie. She was forced to explain to the school that she couldn't take the job after all.

Slowly, Nellie's health improved. In 1863 she moved with her parents to Littleton, a few miles from Westford, where Peter Swallow bought another, bigger store. Nellie once again became his assistant. She kept the accounts, stocked the shelves, and even acted as unofficial postmistress. This last job was her favorite. It allowed her to keep copies of all the latest magazines in an informal lending library.

Nellie was popular among the store's customers, even though she often did unexpected things. Once she surprised the menfolk by refusing to let them light up their pipes in the store. "Why do you sell us tobacco if you don't expect us to smoke it?" they asked. "We sell you molasses, too," said Nellie. "But we don't expect you to stay here and cook it up."

Nellie also had a joke with her customers about biscuits. Some women swore by baking powder for their biscuits, while others insisted saleratus made the biscuits rise higher. The store sold both products—and Nellie knew that both were exactly the same thing, under different names. She would give the baking powder boosters their order from the saleratus jar and listen the next day as they bragged how superior their baking powder biscuits were!

By the time Nellie was twenty-two, her health had improved, the store was doing well, and Nellie's parents made no objection to her taking a teaching job close to home.

The new schoolmistress at East Center School stood just over five feet tall. Her dark hair was parted in the middle and brushed back into a simple bun. Nellie's students knew the chill of those big gray eyes staring down at them when they misbehaved. But more often, they felt the warmth of her wide grin when they did well.

"I call out 30 classes each day," Nellie told cousin Annie. Her "scholars," as she called them, kept her very busy. In her free time, Nellie read books and magazines. On weekends, she went home and helped in the store. By February of 1865, the strain became too much. She did not have the strength to continue both her job as a schoolteacher and her duty to her parents.

Duty won out. Nellie gave up her job and her quiet room in the boardinghouse by the school and returned home.

"I am the same Nellie as of old, full of business, never seeing a leisure hour, never finding time to study or read half as much as I want," Nellie told Annie. Nellie was tired all the time and becoming sad. She was depressed that she was not teaching. She wanted so desperately to be of use to people, to make a difference in the world.

Nellie had her nose buried in a book, as usual, as she walked along the common in the nearby town of Lowell. She had come to attend a free public lecture on science. The last thing on Nellie's mind was the street in front of her, or the old woman in the dusty black dress. Nellie almost bumped into her. Stepping aside, Nellie mumbled an embarrassed apology. But the old woman did not step away. She stared directly into Nellie's gray eyes.

"And YOU . . . ," snorted the woman. "You have a great deal of work to do." The old woman bustled off, leaving Nellie rooted in place.

Nellie never forgot those words. "A great deal of work to do." Yes, she thought, I do.

Nellie sighed, put down the store's account books, and picked up a copy of a popular ladies' magazine. There was an exciting piece of news in the column called "Memoranda on Progress."

"Vassar Female College," it said, "will be opened on September 20, 1865, when the examination of applicants will commence."

Nellie read it again. A college for women, right across the border in upstate New York. Until then, there had been no college for women any closer than Oberlin, in Ohio. Vassar! What a beautiful name. And a real college, not a finishing school where proper young ladies were taught etiquette and stitchery. Would they have courses in science? Nellie wondered. Science was the one thing neither her parents nor the teachers at Westford Academy were equipped to teach her.

Yes, they would teach science at Vassar. Matthew Vassar, who founded the school, was of the unusual and unpopular opinion that God gave women and men the same amount of brains. At Vassar College, women would take the same courses, including science classes, offered at colleges for men.

But Nellie Swallow was not one of the 100 eager young women who were accepted to be in the first class at Vassar College. She was not one of the 3,000 who took the entrance examination. She could not even apply.

Three hundred dollars! Where was she going to get three hundred dollars for tuition?

Nellie knew that she had no time for whining. She had much to do, just as the old lady had told her, if she was ever going to earn three hundred dollars for college.

For two full years, Nellie worked toward her goal. She preserved flowers, she took in sewing, she nursed her mother and their sick neighbors, she waited, and she saved. To all, she presented a cheery face.

But inside, her heart was breaking. "Tired!" she wrote in her diary. "So tired." "Tired, indifferent." "Miserable." "Busy, tired."

Nellie later remembered how frustrated she felt. "I was thwarted and hedged in on every side," she recalled. "It seemed as though God didn't help me a bit and man was doing his best against me and my own heart even turned traitor." Sometimes she thought she would burst.

The best Nellie could do was endure. She became pale and thin. It was such a *long* two years. "Two years in *Purgatory*," she called it.

Finally, the time passed. It was June 1868, and Nellie had her three hundred dollars. Ellen Henrietta Swallow was twenty-six years old, with just enough money to live for one year as a student at Vassar College. With bated breath, she waited for the results of her entrance examination.

Through a Lens

The porter had called her "Miss Swallow." Her new roommate called her "Ellen." But she felt very much like little "Nellie" as she took off her bonnet. She felt awkward and nervous and very, very happy. Vassar College! She was really, finally at Vassar!

Ellen examined her new room. The room itself was plain enough: white walls, a green and red patterned carpet, doors and shutters of dark chestnut. So this was what Vassar looked like.

25

Ellen almost had to pinch herself. Miss Lyman, the principal, told her that her marks on the entrance exam were so high, she would be starting as a junior. That was like skipping two grades. Ellen was relieved, because she only had enough money saved for one year of school.

In the dining hall that evening, Ellen stared at her first Vassar dinner: noodle soup, roast beef, succotash, potatoes, and rhubarb pie. She was much too excited to eat all of this. Ellen looked around the dining room. The other girls at Vassar were so much younger than she was. Their hair flowed down to their waists, as if they had left their dressing tables before they were finished getting ready. Ellen, at twenty-six, in her plain black dress and her smooth bun, felt so mature. She sat a little straighter and finished every bite on her plate.

In her first semester at Vassar, Ellen gained thirteen pounds! (She knew that, because she sneaked down to the cellar to weigh herself on a meat scale. There was nothing, not even herself, that Ellen could resist weighing and measuring.)

This was Ellen's day at Vassar: Up at 6:00 A.M., make the bed, prayer and meditation, then classes till lunch. Eat, study, more classes, exercise outdoors for an hour, then reading and study till dinner. Then quiet time for more reading. To Ellen, it was almost heaven.

"The only trouble here is they won't let us study enough," complained Ellen to her mother. "They are so afraid we shall break down, and you know the reputation of the College is at stake, for the question is, can girls get a degree without injuring their health?"

Every day, Ellen tried to stay as strong and healthy as she could. Not just for herself, but to prove that women could take the strain of a college education. Frail health was an excuse used to keep women out of the classroom. And the fact was, many girls did faint under the pressure of reading essays or answering questions aloud in class.

"The senior who read her essay last night suffered everything almost. She cried over it," Ellen told her mother. "I expected to see her sink through the floor, although she had a fine essay."

Ellen's favorite professor, Miss Maria Mitchell, thought that the students should not be forced to speak before groups and refused to hear her own students read their essays. Professor Mitchell was a great example for the girls at Vassar.

A world-famous astronomer, Maria Mitchell had discovered a comet when she was only Ellen's age. She was the first woman elected to the American Academy of Arts and Sciences. Scientists all over the world wrote to her and asked her opinions. Ellen was awed by her.

This is what Maria Mitchell told her students: "Do not falter because you are women. Personally, I believe in women even more than I do in astronomy. Women must believe in other women."

Some men believe in us too, thought Ellen. The chemistry teacher, Professor Farrar, believed in them. He always said women were ideally suited to chemistry, because they were so exacting and neat. Anyone who could get bread to rise was a chemist in Professor Farrar's book!

Professor Farrar was of the new school of scientific thought—he was an "applied" scientist. He believed that science was of no use unless it improved the world. Ellen agreed with her new professor.

When Professor Farrar set up Vassar's first class in analytical chemistry, Ellen jumped at the chance to study with him. There were only three students in the class: Ellen, her good friend Lizzie Coffin, and Annie Howes.

The three of them searched the college for things to analyze. Baking soda, washing soda, bootblacking, pond water—nothing escaped being measured, weighed, poured into test tubes, or viewed under microscopes. One of Ellen's friends joked that she would analyze the contents of a dustpan.

For her whole first year at Vassar, Ellen seemed to be always looking at something through a lens. She stayed up late at night to look through a telescope at things very far away, and in the daytime peered through a microscope at the things all around her.

In April, near the end of her first school year, Ellen sat down and went over her sums again. She had come to college with three hundred dollars. Tuition and room and board were going to total quite a bit more than Ellen had expected. Nothing she did would make the total come out differently. How was she going to stay at her dear Vassar?

The answer came unexpectedly. One day that spring, there was a knock at the door. The principal, Miss Lyman, wanted to see Ellen.

Oh dear, thought Ellen. What can I have done?

She began going over her week, counting up

her sins. Finally she decided that she hadn't done anything too terrible. Why, she wasn't even in the "bad word fund." Every time one of the girls on her dormitory floor used slang, they had to write their name down and pay a penny. Ellen's name didn't appear on the list once.

Principal Lyman stood as her favorite student entered the office. She could not help but smile. This one worked so hard!

Did Miss Swallow think, wondered Miss Lyman, that she could find the time to teach two young ladies arithmetic? Each would pay five dollars a month. Ellen would be permitted to rise an hour earlier in the morning, to catch up on her studies. Would this be agreeable?

Agreeable? Ellen almost whooped out loud, but of course that wouldn't be proper. Miss Lyman was so worried about being proper. Vassar girls couldn't even go into town by themselves, for fear it might be reported in the papers. It was as if Vassar were under one of Professor Farrar's microscopes. Every girl there was setting an example for every other girl who ever wanted to go to college.

Ellen calmed herself and replied that yes, this would be most agreeable.

For the rest of her college career, Ellen earned a comfortable living as a tutor. Averaging one dollar and fifty cents a day, Ellen made as much as a woman who worked in a factory might make in a week.

Throughout 1869 Ellen studied natural history, astronomy, calculus, German, chemistry, and mathematics. She tutored in German, Latin, and math. Before she knew it, it was March 1870 and time for final exams. Now it was Ellen's turn to stand up and defend her work, out loud, in front of everybody.

Ellen wore a black silk dress with lace sleeves to read her senior essay. The other girls were covered in ribbons and bows, but that just wasn't Ellen's style. "Good luck, Swallow," said Professor Mitchell. (She always called her students by their last names.)

Nervous as she was, Ellen was a complete success. She was trembling as she walked to the podium, but once she got there, a calm descended over her.

"I stood there just as though it had been my business to read essays," she wrote to her mother the next day. "I never felt more cool and collected in my life."

Graduation was in April 1870. At that time, fewer than one percent of women in the United States had college degrees. When Ellen graduated, she once again flew in the face of fashion, wearing a simple white dress and no veil. "I do not see the use of a veil for me," Ellen wrote in her diary. "I never wear one over my face, and I do not want it because it is the fashion."

Professor Farrar watched with pride as his two favorite chemists, Ellen Swallow and Lizzie Coffin, accepted their diplomas. He even jokingly called Ellen "Professor Swallow" and Lizzie "Doctor Coffin." A woman doctor and a woman professor. Ellen liked the sound of Professor Farrar's joke.

Ellen now had both a diploma and an excellent job prospect. She was to teach mathematics and astronomy in Argentina, by personal invitation from the country's president. She went home to Worcester, Massachusetts, where her father had started a new business, and waited to sail away to South America.

Months went by. There was unrest in South America. Ellen worried that the contracts with American teachers would be canceled. She was right; they were. Now Ellen had a college degree and no job at all.

True, she could teach school near Worcester. She could help her father in his business and help her mother at home. But would doing these things really make a difference in the world? Because if Ellen knew one thing about herself, she knew she wanted to make a difference. And that was very hard to do in a world where women simply didn't count for much.

Ellen wrote to a friend from Vassar who now lived in Ohio. "Does Dayton boast any drug stores or the like?" she wrote. "Would it be advisable for me to advertise, think you, for a situation in such a place? I rather want to dip into some science."

She wrote to a firm of chemists in Philadelphia, looking for a job. "We know of no position to which we can direct your attention, although we have heard that female assistance has been employed in apothecary stores," they replied.

She wrote to another firm of chemists, Merrick and Gray of Boston. They, too, were sorry to say that they could not help Miss Swallow. They did suggest, however, that she might study at the Institute of Technology in Boston.

Ellen was by now convinced that she wanted to pursue a career in chemistry. But she had never thought about the Massachusetts Institute of Technology, the school Merrick and Gray talked about in their letter.

MIT, as it was called, was founded in 1865, the same year as Vassar. When the school opened, there were only fifteen students in two rooms. Soon it moved to larger quarters and became known throughout New England for its science courses. It was one of the only schools in the country that specialized in applied science — science used for practical purposes.

MIT was too new to have written up all its by-laws. No one ever wrote down "We do not admit women." So when an application was received from one Ellen Henrietta Swallow, the admissions committee didn't quite know what to do with it. No woman had ever been admitted to a scientific school in the United States before.

On December 3, 1870, the committee members looked long and hard at Ellen's application and did the only thing they could think of. They voted unanimously to "postpone the question of the admission of female students until the next meeting."

As it happened, the president of MIT, Dr. John Runkle, knew and admired both Professor Mitchell and Professor Farrar. Armed with their strong recommendations, he urged the committee to take on one special female student.

When Ellen was informed that she would be admitted to MIT without any charge whatsoever, she thought Dr. Runkle was the kindest man on the face of the earth. Afterward, she found out he recommended Ellen be admitted without fees so that, if she was a disaster, the school could claim she wasn't a real student at all.

Ellen tucked her luggage in the corner of her room at 523 Columbus Avenue, Boston. "To be the first woman to enter Massachusetts Institute of Technology, and so far as I know any scientific school," Ellen reflected, "and to do it by myself alone, unaided." She was proud of herself and her achievement.

Ellen fixed breakfast for the landlady's husband (the chore was part of her rent) and set off for her new school. Truly, she was a pioneer on a new frontier.

Dr. Runkle himself greeted Ellen as she arrived at MIT. He introduced Ellen to the only other woman at the Institute—Mrs. Stinson, the assistant in charge of the chemical storeroom. Ellen politely shook hands, but could not wait to see the laboratories and classrooms. Mrs. Stinson and Dr. Runkle stared at her retreating back as Ellen disappeared down the hallway.

"She looks rather frail to take such a difficult course," said Mrs. Stinson.

"Yes, but did you notice her eyes?" asked Dr. Runkle. "They are steadfast and they are courageous. She will not fail."

Beakers &
Broken Suspenders

As usual, the male students stepped aside and let Ellen walk by. No one stopped to talk. Ellen sometimes felt as if she were some strange, alien creature at MIT. She was given a desk far away from the other students, and the best she could do was smile and study and wait for things to change.

Slowly, things did begin to change. Ellen wrote to her mother: "Last night Prof. B found me useful to mend his suspenders which had come to grief, much to the amusement of young Mr. C. I try to keep all sorts of things such as needles, thread, pins, scissors, etc., round, and they are getting to come to me for everything they want."

Ellen discovered that by doing the things people expected of a woman, she was making friends and "allies" at MIT. Plus, she found, by being "useful in a decidedly general way, they can't say *study* spoils me for anything else." Gradually, this dangerous woman who dared to enter a man's world didn't look so dangerous after all.

Ellen was convinced that you could catch more flies with honey than with vinegar. For the rest of her time at MIT, Ellen was the one everyone went to with emergencies, from a cut finger to a mathematical equation that didn't come out right.

But Ellen wasn't always a success in winning over the male staff at MIT. Professor Nichols, Ellen's instructor in analytical chemistry, still didn't think that women should be allowed to study advanced science. The young mineralogy teacher, Robert Richards, however, was very impressed with Ellen Swallow.

Professor Richards was impressed with Ellen's accurate analyses of the rocks and minerals he brought to class from his expeditions. He was impressed with her curiosity and quick intelligence. He was impressed with her bright eyes. He was impressed with . . . well, he was impressed with everything about her.

One day Ellen was sitting, lost in thought, during the two-hour journey from Boston back to her parents' house. She was worried about her mother's health, and she wanted to talk to her father about using her chemistry to help in his business. Peter Swallow was manufacturing artificial building stone—something like concrete—and had asked his daughter to be his partner.

Before Ellen had a chance to sit down and talk with her mother, a man from the railroad station came to the door. He stood with his head bowed and his hat in his hands. There was bad news, he said. Ellen's father had been horribly injured in an accident.

Peter Swallow lingered for four days, feverish and in pain, on a daybed in the living room. Then he died.

Heartbroken, Fanny Swallow would not leave her home and move to Boston with her daughter. For many months, Ellen traveled four hours a day, back and forth, from Worcester to Boston. She could not leave her mother all alone.

Between her studies, extra work in the chemistry lab, and her time with her mother, Ellen seldom slept more than four hours a night. She tried to make time for the handsome young professor

Richards, but it was difficult. "I wish I were trip-lets," she sighed. She made up ways to save min-utes and seconds. She even invented her own shorthand, to write notes and letters faster.

In June 1873 Ellen Swallow became the first woman in America to earn a degree in chemistry. She became the first woman to graduate from the Massachusetts Institute of Technology. And Robert Hallowell Richards asked her to marry him.

When he first asked her, Ellen joked that she could never marry a man who smoked. Robert quit smoking. Then she said she had to finish a series of experiments. She finished her experi-ments. Next she wanted to set up science classes for the Women's Education Association, so that other girls could follow the trail she had blazed.

It was all very important work. So much to do! Still, Ellen knew she was running out of excuses.

Fanny couldn't understand why Ellen didn't rush to marry this tall, slow-talking New Englander. "Your professor," was what Fanny called him.

Ellen wasn't sure what to do. Yes, she was happy when she was around Bobby. She liked his brother, Henry, and his sister-in-law, Laura. (Laura Richards, a well-known poet, made up the name "Ellencyclopedia" for Bobby's clever friend.)

But to marry and give up her dreams?

For two years, Robert Richards courted the serious-minded Ellen Swallow. Finally, Ellen came to understand that Robert did not want her to trade in her dreams for a dustpan and cookstove. He wanted the two of them to be pioneers, facing the future together. Finally, Ellen said "Yes." At Union Chapel, on a sunny June day in 1875, she became Mrs. Robert Hallowell Richards.

Robert Richards was from an old and prominent Maine family. He was a respected mining engineer. He was thirty years old. Yet when he married Ellen Swallow, he was so flustered that he forgot to bring a change of clothes to wear home. Ellen laughed at him, stuck in his white wedding tie, until she realized she had left the keys to their new home back in her room on Columbus Avenue!

The Richardses' house at 32 Eliot Street in Jamaica Plain, just outside of Boston, was different from other houses of its day. Instead of heavy curtains, Ellen put green plants in her windows. She pulled up the thick, dusty carpets. Ellen always said that heavy carpets were actually harmful to one's health, full of dirt and germs. She replaced them with colorful area rugs on a polished wooden floor.

She and Robert designed a hood for the stove to keep polluted air out of the house. They designed a ventilator for the gas lighting, and they put in a skylight. Robert had a gas meter installed in their kitchen, and Ellen made a study of how much energy was needed to cook different foods.

After all, they were scientists. What were they to do, leave science at the lab every evening when they went home? No. As applied scientists, they wanted to apply science to their daily lives.

Once Ellen graduated from MIT, the Institute no longer had a single female student. Ellen's example alone was not enough to open the doors of chemistry to all women. But she was able to open one door to some women.

There was a run-down old building in back of the Institute, a workshop that no one used. By volunteering to raise the money for the equipment, to teach for no pay, and to keep the place clean herself, Ellen was able to convince the Institute to turn the building into a chemistry lab for women.

The Woman's Laboratory (or "the Dump," as everyone called it) opened in November 1876. Ellen Richards, who founded it, was appointed assistant director. A male professor was made director.

Twenty-three women enrolled as special students in chemistry. Ellen was professor, confessor, big sister, and mother hen to all the female students at the Dump. Her husband, Robert, joked that Ellen was the dean of women, only without the title and without the pay.

At the end of one year, the professors at MIT saw something amazing in the Woman's Laboratory. They saw that women who took the same chemistry courses as men were just as likely to pass the courses as men. And not only did they pass the courses, but they did it without getting faint and weak and sick.

The Institute was impressed. But not impressed enough to provide the money for the Woman's Laboratory to operate a second year. Ellen and the Women's Education Association had to raise the money, penny by penny, from women in the community.

After the Woman's Laboratory and its students studied and succeeded for a second year, the Institute decided it had better uses for the Dump. They needed the space for male students. But the women hadn't done anything to give the Institute an excuse to kick them out. They deserved a place to study.

The governing committee thought and thought and soon came up with an answer. In 1878 the Woman's Laboratory was torn down and replaced with a new, larger chemistry lab for the regular students of MIT. And from 1878 on, anyone—male or female—who had passed the entrance tests and paid the necessary fee could enter MIT as a regular student. The door that Ellen had stuck her foot through eight years before was finally staying open.

But there were still some who did not wish to see a woman succeed in science. After working very hard for two years at MIT to get a doctorate, the most advanced degree the school offered, Ellen was turned down with no explanation. When she heard the news, she was angry and heartsick.

Robert talked to some of his friends at the Institute and told Ellen the sad story. The heads of the chemistry department simply did not want to award the department's first doctorate degree to a woman. This was one door Ellen could not open.

4

Under Water!

The first professional woman chemist in America was in her laboratory at MIT analyzing a sack of groceries that one of her students gathered from local stores. Ellen shook up her test tubes and peered through her microscope. A greedy shopkeeper had loaded the sugar with sand and was using yellow dye to make the milk look as if it had more cream in it than it really did. There were no laws to stop people from doing any of this.

And people wondered what good chemistry would do a woman, laughed Ellen. Well, it would keep her from baking a cake with sand, for one. Maybe it would save the lives of her husband or her children!

In the late 1800s, people still found it hard to believe that invisible "germs" and "bacteria" caused diseases. When people got sick and died, it was hard to see what it had to do with open sewers or closed-up houses. How could air and water that looked perfectly clear and clean hurt them? people wondered. Yet thousands died every year from polluted water and foul air.

Ellen Richards knew all too well about the dangers of bad water and air. Her husband, Robert, was sick for nearly two years with typhoid fever, one of many diseases spread by dirty water. And, Ellen said to herself, we haven't even begun to talk about the dangers of bad food!

Using chemistry to improve people's health was becoming Ellen's specialty. In 1884 Ellen became an instructor at MIT's new sanitary chemistry lab, a pioneer program in using chemistry to improve public health. Perhaps because her mother had always been frail, or perhaps because she herself had been so weak and sickly at one time, Ellen thought one of science's goals should be to make people healthier. If they were healthier, they'd be more productive. And if people were more productive, Ellen was convinced they would also be happier.

So Ellen was particularly excited when she was approached for an important scientific study. The Massachusetts Board of Health wanted to make the first statewide study of water pollution in the United States.

Officials had come to believe that polluted water was harming the people of Massachusetts. We want to do something about it, they decided. But how can we do something about polluted water unless we know which water is polluted? We need to test all the water in the state! And what's more, we need some scale, some way to judge the water against a standard of purity.

The Board of Health asked MIT to do this study, to find this water standard. The senior scientist was to be an MIT professor named Dr. Drown, and the only person he wanted assisting him was Ellen Richards. No one else was as precise, as accurate in her work.

At the time, the usual method for testing the purity of water was to inject some under the skin of a rabbit. If the water was infected, the rabbit would get sick. This test was not only crude and time-consuming, it was also cruel to the rabbit. Ellen wanted to find a way to analyze water chemically.

She and Dr. Drown went over different possibilities. They looked at nitrates and nitrites, two chemicals found in water when bacteria are present. Measuring the amount of nitrates and nitrites was an idea Ellen had tried once before, when she and Dr. Nichols had done a much smaller water study back in her student days.

This was a fine method to see if one stream or one pond was polluted. But what Ellen and Dr. Drown needed was a new method, a way to test pollution in all the lakes and rivers of the state. They needed to make a chart against which all water could be judged.

Ellen and Dr. Drown discussed the chemicals found in water when it was polluted, and when it was safe. Finally they hit on an idea: chlorine.

Chlorine is one substance that does not break down in water. If there is too much chlorine in a water sample, it is there for a reason. One reason can be that the water is polluted. Another reason can be that the water is close to the ocean. (No one added chlorine to water as a disinfectant in the 1800s.)

All Ellen needed to do was test the amount of chlorine in water from all over the state and mark how near or how far that water was to the ocean.

Then they would have a map, a chart, a way to measure water anywhere in Massachusetts and see if it was safe to drink.

"I have been *under water* since June 1 of last year," laughed Ellen to a friend. "And I suppose it will be the same for another year. We are testing all the public supplies once a month, and we are up to twenty-five hundred samples already."

Ellen tested water from every lake and river in Massachusetts. She worked fourteen hours a day, often seven days a week. If it got too hot to work in the daytime, she worked at night. Every test tube had to be rinsed with distilled water and every tabletop and piece of equipment had to be spotless. It was painstaking work. Before the survey was completed, more than 40,000 samples had been analyzed, most of them by Ellen herself.

When it was all over, Massachusetts had the first "Normal Chlorine Map" in the world. It let people in any town tell instantly if there was something wrong with their water. It was the first standard for fresh water anywhere. And it was all made possible, wrote Dr. Drown, "mainly due to Mrs. Richards' great zeal and vigilance."

⑤

A Good, Hot Lunch

By the mid-1880s, Ellen Richards had become one of the top chemists in the country. Corporations hired her to test water supplies. (She often tested the water at schools and orphanages for free.) Mine owners hired her to analyze their ore. A national insurance company hired her to find out which machine oils caused the most fires in factories. Companies set their insurance rates by Ellen's findings.

Ellen was, she had always said, "one whose aim is to do all of the good she can in the world, and not to be one of those delicate little dolls or the silly fools who make up the bulk of American women, slaves to society and fashion."

In 1885 Ellen had been offered the job of superintendent of the Boston schools. She turned it down because, as she explained to a friend, "a political place with no power, only influence, is not to my taste."

Even though Ellen would not accept the position of superintendent of schools, the Board of Education soon came to her with another most interesting offer. The board had asked if she could create a hot lunch program for the children. Could she plan a balanced, healthy meal for all the students in the Boston schools?

Ellen and Robert both believed in the phrase "you are what you eat." In their home they ate lots of fresh fruits and vegetables, whole-grain breads, and lean meats. In the late 1800s and early 1900s, most people ate rich sauces and gooey pastries. Ellen said these people were digging their graves with their knives and forks. She wanted to teach people about new ideas like "calories" and "albuminoids" (called "proteins" today).

Ellen's ideas were not quickly accepted. At one time she helped create an experimental health food kitchen, and she never forgot the comment of one stubborn woman who visited the place. "I don't want to eat what's good for me," said the woman. "I'd ruther eat what I'd ruther."

Throughout Massachusetts, schoolchildren were eating whatever they'd "ruther," since there was no lunch served in public schools. Janitors set up shop in school basements and peddled snacks to the kids. The janitors cared only about what sold best, not about good nutrition. The typical school lunch was cake and candy. Children who had no money went hungry.

Providing nutritious meals for the children seemed like such a simple and good idea. Who would have thought it would be so difficult to do? Ellen sighed, "I believe I'd feel safer stepping into a nest of vipers than I do when my recommendations threaten someone else's profits."

This time Ellen's ideas threatened Boston's school janitors. They weren't at all happy about seeing their extra income disappear. When Ellen and her co-workers tried to bring hot lunches into the schools, the janitors did everything possible to stop them. The keys to the lunchroom would be "lost." Pots and pans would go "missing." Helpers would unexpectedly turn up "sick."

But despite the janitors' sabotage, the school lunch program was a success. Before the year was out, five thousand students a day were eating a healthy, filling meal. The Boston school lunch program became a model for the whole country. (Although even today, we'd sometimes "ruther eat what we'd ruther!")

⑥

Working for Women

Ellen continued to work for the public good: clean water, fresh air, pure food. And in her "playtime," as she called it, she worked for women, just as she had done at the Woman's Laboratory.

Not only do women have to be brought to science, she thought. Science has to be brought to women, wherever they might be.

For twenty-five years Ellen worked with Studies at Home, a correspondence school for women.

Ellen's courses brought botany, geology, and mineralogy to women stuck in kitchens, nurseries, and sickrooms around the country. She answered thousands of letters by hand, sent rock and plant samples, and encouraged her students. Every letter Ellen closed with the phrase "keep thinking."

When she wasn't writing to women students at home, she was out in cities and towns giving lectures and encouraging talks. Educating women in the basics of science was a new idea. After all, "What good is science to a woman?" people still asked.

One day in 1879, Ellen got a chance to answer that question in front of a room of three hundred women. It was in Poughkeepsie, New York, not far from Vassar College. Maria Mitchell, Ellen's old astronomy professor, was there to hear the talk. ("I discovered Mrs. Richards," Mitchell told everybody.) Ellen's voice was strong and clear, as usual, when she said:

Now it is often stated that our educational system unfits girls for their work in life, which is largely that of housekeepers. It cannot be the knowledge which unfits them. One can never know too much of the things which one is to handle. Can a railroad engineer know too much about the parts of his engine? Can the cotton manufacturer know too much about the cotton fiber? Can a cook know too much about the composition and nutritive value of the meats and vegetables she uses? Can a housekeeper know too much about the effect of fresh air on the human system, of the dangers of sewer gas, of foul water?

Ellen made thousands of such speeches over the years. She wrote books on clean air, pure water, and healthy foods.

In 1908 Ellen Richards was elected the first president of the American Home Economics Association, a group determined to bring modern science into old-fashioned homes. And in 1910 Ellen finally became *Dr.* Richards when she was awarded her doctor of science degree by Smith, a women's college.

In March 1911 Ellen was giving a talk entitled "Is the Increased Cost of Living a Sign of Social Advance?" when she began to feel terrible pains in her chest. She did not want to worry Robert, so she said nothing to him. But the pain would not go away.

A few days later, Ellen told Robert she had decided to bring some work home with her from the Institute. She was fine, she said. She just needed some rest. Finally she let Robert call a doctor. The diagnosis was heart disease.

Ellen Swallow Richards died peacefully in the late evening of March 30, 1911. She was sixty-eight years old. The man who knew her best summed up her life and work as well as anyone could. This is the epitaph Robert Richards had inscribed on his wife's tombstone:

Pioneer — Educator — Scientist
An Earnest Seeker — A Tireless Worker
A Thoughtful Friend — A Helper of Mankind

And always, an adventurous spirit.

Bibliography

Ellen Swallow Richards was a very busy woman, yet she took the time to write thousands of letters and to keep a diary. All of the quoted text in this book comes from material written by Ellen herself, or written down by her friends and family. The major source on Ellen Richards, the biography by friend and former student Caroline Hunt, includes large excerpts from Ellen's diaries.

Clarke, Robert. *Ellen Swallow: The Woman Who Founded Ecology.* Chicago: Follett Publishing Co., 1973.

Douty, Esther M. *America's First Woman Chemist.* New York: Julian Messner, 1961.

Hunt, Caroline. *The Life of Ellen H. Richards.* Boston: Whitcomb and Barrows, 1912.

Richards, Robert H. *Robert Hallowell Richards: His Mark.* Boston: Little, Brown, 1936.

Stern, Madeleine B. *We the Women: Career Firsts of Nineteenth-Century America.* New York: Schulte Publishing Co., 1963.

Yost, Edna. *American Women of Science.* Philadelphia: Frederick A. Stokes Co., 1943.